The Abolition Of Slavery
The Right Of The Government Under The War Power

by

Ed. William Lloyd Garrison

**The Abolition Of Slavery
The Right Of The Government Under
The War Power
by Ed. William Lloyd Garrison**

Copyright © 2023

All Rights reserved.

No part of this publication may be reproduced,
stored in a retrieval system, or transmitted in any
form or by any means, electronic, mechanical,
photocopying or Otherwise, without the written
permission of the publisher.
The author/editor asserts the moral right to
be identified as the author/editor of this work.

ISBN: 978-93-59957-43-2

Published by

DOUBLE 9 BOOKS

2/13-B, Ansari Road
Daryaganj, New Delhi – 110002
info@double9books.com
www.double9books.com
Tel. 011-40042856

This book is under public domain

ABOUT THE EDITOR

" The Abiding Presence of the Holy Ghost inside the Soul" is a profound spiritual painting by Bede Jarrett, an English Dominican friar and theologian. This e-book, first published in the early twentieth century, addresses the deep relationship between the human soul and the Holy Spirit, focusing on Christian theology and mysticism. Bede Jarrett's study looks into the theological concept of the Holy Spirit indwelling the believer's soul. He highlights the divine presence's transformational power, emphasizing its function in guiding, soothing, and sanctifying the individual's non secular path. The book takes readers on a deep and serious journey through the Christian religion and the amazing reviews that can come with it. Bede Jarrett's writing is distinguished by its religious vision and eloquence, making it accessible to both theologians and those seeking a greater understanding of their faith. "The Abiding Presence of the Holy Spirit within the Soul" is an invitation to discover the profound and transformational relationship between the person and the supernatural. It invites readers to reflect on their spiritual studies as well as the role of the Holy Spirit in their life, promoting a sense of connection and communion with the divine.

CONTENTS

EMANCIPATION UNDER THE WAR POWER

Extracts from the speech of John Quincy Adams, delivered in the U.S. House of Representatives, April 14 and 15, 1842, on War with Great Britain and Mexico:—

What I say is involuntary, because the subject has been brought into the House from another quarter, as the gentleman himself admits. I would leave that institution to the exclusive consideration and management of the States more peculiarly interested in it, just as long as they can keep within their own bounds. So far, I admit that Congress has no power to meddle with it. As long as they do not step out of their own bounds, and do not put the question to the people of the United States, whose peace, welfare and happiness are all at stake, so long I will agree to leave them to themselves. But when a member from a free State brings forward certain resolutions, for which, instead of reasoning to disprove his positions, you vote a censure upon him, and that without hearing, it is quite another affair. At the time this was done, I said that, as far as I could understand the resolutions proposed by the gentleman from Ohio, (Mr. Giddings,) there were some of them for which I was ready to vote, and some which I must vote against; and I will now tell this House, my constituents, and the world of mankind, that the resolution against which I would have voted was that in which he declares that what are called the slave States have the exclusive right of consultation on the subject of slavery. For that resolution I never would vote, because I believe that it is not just, and does not contain constitutional doctrine. I believe that, so long as the slave States are able to sustain their institutions without going abroad or calling upon other parts of the Union to aid them or act on the subject, so long I will consent never to interfere. I have said this, and I repeat it; but if they come to the free States, and say to them, you must help us to keep down our slaves, you must aid us in an insurrection and a civil war, then I say that with that call comes a full and plenary power to this House and to the Senate over the whole subject. It is a war power. I say it is a war power, and when your country is actually in war, whether it be a war of invasion or a war of insurrection, Congress has power to carry on the war, and must carry it on, according to the laws of war; and by the laws of war, an invaded country has all its laws and municipal institutions swept by the board, and martial law takes the place of them. This power in Congress has, perhaps, never been called into exercise under the present Constitution of the United States. But when the laws of war are in force, what, I ask, is one of those laws? It is this: that when a country is invaded, and two hostile armies are set in martial array, the commanders of both armies have power to emancipate all the slaves in the invaded territory. Nor is this a mere theoretic statement. The history of South America shows that the doctrine has been carried into practical execution within the last thirty years. Slavery was abolished in Columbia, first, by the Spanish General Morillo, and, secondly, by the American General Bolivar. It was abolished by virtue of a military command given at the head of the army, and its abolition continues to be law to this day. It was abolished by the laws of war, and not by municipal enactments; the power was exercised by military commanders, under instructions, of course, from their respective Governments. And here I recur again to the example of Gen. Jackson. What are you now about in Congress? You are about passing a grant to refund to Gen. Jackson the amount of a certain fine imposed upon him by a Judge, under the laws of the State of Louisiana. You are going to refund him the money, with interest; and this you are going to do because the imposition of the fine was unjust. And why was it unjust? Because Gen. Jackson was acting under the laws of war, and because the moment you place a military commander in a district which is the theatre of war, the laws of war apply to that district.

I might furnish a thousand proofs to show that the pretensions of gentlemen to the sanctity of their municipal institutions under a state of actual invasion and of actual war, whether servile, civil or foreign, is wholly unfounded, and that the laws of war do, in all such cases, take the precedence. I lay this down as the law of nations. I say that military authority takes, for the time, the place of all municipal institutions, and slavery among the rest; and that, under that state of things, so far from its being true that the States where slavery exists have the exclusive management of the subject, not only the President of the United States, but the Commander of the Army, has power to order the universal emancipation of the slaves. I have given here more in detail a principle which I have asserted on this floor before now, and of which I have no more doubt than that you, sir, occupy that chair. I give it in its development, in order that any gentleman from any part of the Union may, if he thinks proper, deny the truth of the position, and may maintain his denial; not by indignation, not by passion and fury, but by sound and sober reasoning from the laws of nations and the laws of war. And if my position can be answered and refuted, I shall receive the refutation with pleasure; I shall be glad to listen to reason, aside, as I say, from indignation and passion. And if, by the force of reasoning, my understanding can be convinced, I here pledge myself to recant what I have asserted.

Let my position be answered; let me be told, let my constituents be told, the people of my State be told—a State whose soil tolerates not the foot of a slave—that they are bound by the Constitution to a long and toilsome march under burning summer suns and a deadly Southern clime for the suppression of a servile war; that they are bound to leave their bodies to rot upon the sands of Carolina, to leave their wives widows and their children orphans; that those who cannot march are bound to pour out their treasures while their sons or brothers are pouring out their blood to suppress a servile, combined with a civil or a foreign war, and yet that there exists no power beyond the limits of the slave State where such war is raging to emancipate the slaves. I say, let this be proved—I am open to conviction; but till that conviction comes, I put it forth not as a dictate of feeling, but as a settled maxim of the laws of nations, that, in such a case, the military supersedes the civil power; and on this account I should have been obliged to vote, as I have said, against one of the resolutions of my excellent friend from Ohio, (Mr. Giddings,) or should at least have required that it be amended in conformity with the Constitution of the United States.

THE WAR POWER OVER SLAVERY

We published, not long ago, an extract from a speech delivered by John Quincy Adams in Congress in 1842, in which that eminent statesman confidently announced the doctrine, that in a state of war, civil or servile, in the Southern States, Congress has full and plenary power over the whole subject of slavery; martial law takes the place of civil laws and municipal institutions, slavery among the rest, and "not only the President of the United States, but the Commander of the Army, has power to order the universal emancipation of the slaves."

Mr. Adams was, in 1842, under the ban of the slaveholders, who were trying to censure him or expel him from the House for presenting a petition in favor of the dissolution of the Union. Lest it may be thought that the doctrine announced at this time was thrown out hastily and offensively, and for the purpose of annoying and aggravating his enemies, and without due consideration, it may be worth while to show that six years previous, in May, 1836, Mr. Adams held the same opinions, and announced them as plainly as in 1842. Indeed, it is quite likely that this earlier announcement of these views was the cause of the secret hostility to the ex-President, which broke out so rancorously in 1842. We have before us a speech by Mr. Adams, on the joint resolution for distributing rations to the distressed fugitives from Indian hostilities in the States of Alabama and Georgia, delivered in the House of Representatives, May 25, 1836, and published at the office of the National Intelligencer. We quote from it the following classification of the powers of Congress and the Executive:—

"There are, then, Mr. Chairman, in the authority of Congress and of the Executive, two classes of powers, altogether different in their nature, and often incompatible with each other—the war power and the peace power. The peace power is limited by regulations and restricted by provisions prescribed within the Constitution itself. The war power is limited only by the laws and usages of nations. This power is tremendous: it is strictly constitutional, but it breaks down every barrier so anxiously erected for the protection of liberty, of property, and of life. This, sir, is the power which authorizes you to pass the resolution now before you, and, in my opinion, no other."

After an interruption, Mr. Adams returned to this subject, and went on to say:—

"There are, indeed, powers of peace conferred upon Congress which also come within the scope and jurisdiction of the laws of nations, such as the negotiation of treaties of amity and commerce, the interchange of public ministers and consuls, and all the personal and social intercourse between the individual inhabitants of the United States and foreign nations, and the Indian tribes, which require the interposition of any law. But the powers of war are all regulated by the laws of nations, and are subject to no other limitation...It was upon this principle that I voted against the resolution reported by the slavery committee, 'that Congress possess no constitutional authority to interfere, in any way, with the institution of slavery in any of the States of this Confederacy,' to which resolution most of those with whom I usually concur, and even my own colleagues in this House, gave their assent. I do not admit that there is, even among the peace powers of Congress, no such authority; but in war, there are many ways by which Congress not only have the authority, but ARE BOUND TO INTERFERE WITH THE INSTITUTION OF SLAVERY IN THE STATES. The existing law prohibiting the importation of slaves into the United States from foreign countries is itself an interference with the institution of slavery in the States. It was so considered by the founders of the Constitution of the United States, in which it was stipulated that Congress should not interfere, in that way, with the institution, prior to the year 1808.

"During the late war with Great Britain, the military and naval commanders of that nation issued proclamations, inviting the slaves to repair to their standard, with promises of freedom and of settlement in some of the British colonial establishments. This surely was an interference with the institution of slavery in the States. By the treaty of peace, Great Britain stipulated to evacuate all the forts and places in the United States, without carrying away any slaves. If the Government of the United States had no power to interfere, in any way, with the institution of slavery in the States, they would not have had the authority to require this stipulation. It is well known that this engagement was not fulfilled by the British naval and military commanders; that, on the contrary, they did carry away all the slaves whom they had induced to join them, and that the British Government inflexibly refused to restore any of them to their masters; that a claim of indemnity was consequently instituted in behalf of the owners of the slaves, and was successfully maintained. All that series of transactions was an interference by Congress with the institution of slavery in the States in one way—in the way of protection and support. It was by the institution of slavery alone that the restitution of slaves, enticed by proclamations into the British service, could be claimed as property. But for the institution of slavery, the British commanders could neither have allured them to their standard, nor restored them otherwise than as liberated prisoners of war. But for the institution of slavery, there could have been no stipulation that they should not be carried away as property, nor any claim of indemnity for the violation of that engagement."

If this speech had been made in 1860 instead of 1836, Mr. Adams would not have been compelled to rely upon these comparatively trivial and unimportant instances of interference by Congress and the President for the support and protection of slavery. For the last twenty years, the support and protection of that institution has been, to use Mr. Adams's words at a later day, the vital and animating spirit of the Government; and the Constitution has been interpreted and administered as if it contained an injunction upon all men, in power and out of power, to sustain and perpetuate slavery. Mr. Adams goes on to state how the war power may be used:—

"But the war power of Congress over the institution of slavery in the States is yet far more extensive. Suppose the case of a servile war, complicated, as to some extent it is even now, with an Indian war; suppose Congress were called to raise armies, to supply money from the whole Union to suppress a servile insurrection: would they have no authority to interfere with the institution of slavery? The issue of a servile war may be disastrous; it may become necessary for the master of the slave to recognize his emancipation by a treaty of peace; can it for an instant be pretended that Congress, in such a contingency, would have no authority to interfere with the institution of slavery, in any way, in the States? Why, it would be equivalent to saying that Congress have no constitutional authority to make peace. I suppose a more portentous case, certainly within the bounds of possibility—I would to God I could say, not within the bounds of probability—"

Mr. Adams here, at considerable length, portrays the danger then existing of a war with Mexico, involving England and the European powers, bringing hostile armies and fleets to our own Southern territory, and inducing not only a foreign war, but an Indian, a civil, and a servile war, and making of the Southern States "the battle-field upon which the last great conflict will be fought between Slavery and Emancipation." "Do you imagine (he asks) that your Congress will have no constitutional authority to interfere with the institution of slavery, in any way, in the States of this Confederacy? Sir, they must and will interfere with it—perhaps to sustain it by war, perhaps to abolish it by treaties of peace; and they will not only possess the constitutional power so to interfere, but they will be bound in duty to do it, by the express provisions of the Constitution itself. From the instant that your slaveholding States become the theatre of a war, civil, servile, or foreign, from that instant, the war powers of Congress extend to interference with the institution of slavery, in every way by which it can be interfered with, from a claim of indemnity for slaves taken or destroyed, to the cession of States burdened with slavery to a foreign power."—New York Tribune.

THE WAR IN ITS RELATION TO SLAVERY.

To THE EDITOR OF THE NEW YORK TRIBUNE:

SIR,—Our country is opening up a new page in the history of governments. The world has never witnessed such a spontaneous uprising of any people in support of free institutions as that now exhibited by the citizens of our Northern States. I observe that the vexed question of slavery still has to be met, both in the Cabinet and in the field. It has been met by former Presidents, by former Cabinets, and by former military officers. They have established a train of precedents that may be well followed at this day. I write now for the purpose of inviting attention to those principles of international law which are regarded by publicists and jurists as proper guides in the exercise of that despotic and almost unlimited authority called the "war power." A synopsis of these doctrines was given by Major General Gaines, at New Orleans, in 1838.

General Jessup had captured many fugitive slaves and Indians in Florida, and had ordered them to be sent west of the Mississippi. At New Orleans, they were claimed by the owners, under legal process; but Gen. Gaines, commanding that military district, refused to deliver them to the sheriff, and appeared in court, stating his own defence.

He declared that these people (men, women and children) were captured in wars and held as prisoners of war: that as commander of that military department or district, he held them subject only to the order of the National Executive: that he could recognize no other power in time of war, or by the laws of war, as authorized to take prisoners from his possession.

He asserted that, in time of war, all slaves were belligerents as much as their masters. The slave men, said he, cultivate the earth and supply provisions. The women cook the food, nurse the wounded and sick, and contribute to the maintenance of the war, often more than the same number of males. The slave children equally contribute whatever they are able to the support of the war. Indeed, he well supported General Butler's declaration, that slaves are contraband of war.

The military officer, said he, can enter into no judicial examination of the claim of one man to the bone and muscle of another as property. Nor could he, as a military officer, know what the laws of Florida were while engaged in maintaining the Federal Government by force of arms. In such case, he could only be guided by the laws of war; and whatever may be the laws of any State, they must yield to the safety of the Federal Government. This defence of General Gaines may be found in House Document No. 225, of the Second Session of the 25th Congress. He sent the slaves West, where they became free.

Louis, the slave of a man named Pacheco, betrayed Major Dade's battalion, in 1836, and when he had witnessed their massacre, he joined the enemy. Two years subsequently, he was captured, Pacheco claimed him; General Jessup said if he had time, he would try him before a court-martial and hang him, but would not deliver him to any man. He however sent him West, and the fugitive slave became a free man, and is now fighting the Texans. General Jessup reported his action to the War Department, and Mr. Van Buren, then President, with his Cabinet, approved it. Pacheco then appealed to Congress, asking that body to pay him for the loss of his slave; and Mr. Greeley will recollect that he and myself, and a majority of the House of Representatives, voted against the bill, which was rejected. All concurred in the opinion that General Jessup did right in emancipating the slave, instead of returning him to his master.

In 1838, General Taylor captured a number of negroes said to be fugitive slaves. Citizens of Florida, learning what had been done, immediately gathered around his camp, intending to secure the slaves who had escaped from them. General Taylor told them that he had no prisoners but "prisoners of war." The claimants then desired to look at them, in order to determine whether he was holding their slaves as prisoners. The veteran warrior replied that no man should examine his prisoners for such a purpose; and he ordered them to depart. This action being reported to the War Department, was approved by the Executive. The slaves, however, were sent West, and set free.

In 1836, General Jessup wanted guides and men to act as spies. He therefore engaged several fugitive slaves to act as such, agreeing to secure the freedom of themselves and families if they served the Government faithfully. They agreed to do so, fulfilled their agreement, were sent West, and set free. Mr. Van Buren's Administration approved the contract, and Mr. Tyler's Administration approved the manner in which General Jessup fulfilled it by setting the slaves free.

In December, 1814, General Jackson impressed a large number of slaves at and near New Orleans, and kept them at work erecting defences, behind which his troops won such glory on the 8th of January, 1815. The masters remonstrated. Jackson disregarded their remonstrances, and kept the slaves at work until many of them were killed by the enemy's shots; yet his action was approved by Mr. Madison and Cabinet, and by Congress, which has ever refused to pay the masters for their losses.

But in all these cases, the masters were professedly friends of the Government; and yet our Presidents and Cabinets and Generals have not hesitated to emancipate their slaves whenever in time of war it was supposed to be for the interest of the country to do so. This was done in the exercise of the "war power" to which Mr. Adams referred in Congress, and for which he had the most abundant authority. But I think no records of this nation, nor of any other nation, will show an instance in which a fugitive slave has been sent back to a master who was in rebellion against the very Government who held his slave as captive.

From these precedents I deduce the following doctrines:—

1. That slaves belonging to an enemy are now and have ever been regarded as belligerents; may be lawfully captured and set free, sent out of the State, or otherwise disposed of at the will of the Executive.

2. That as slaves enable an enemy to continue and carry on the war now waged against our Government, it becomes the duty of all officers and loyal citizens to use every proper means to induce the slaves to leave their masters, and cease lending aid and comfort to the rebels.

3. That in all cases it becomes the duty of the Executive, and of all Executive officers and loyal citizens, to aid, assist and encourage those slaves who have escaped from rebel masters to continue their flight and maintain their liberty.

4. That to send back a fugitive slave to a rebel master would be lending aid and assistance to the rebellion. That those who arrest and send back

such fugitives identify themselves with the enemies of our Government, and should be indicted as traitors.

J. R. GIDDINGS.

MONTREAL, June 6, 1861.

Accordingly, let old Virginia begin to put her house in order, and pack up for the removal of her half million of slaves, for fear of the impending storm. She has invited it, and only a speedy repentance will save her from being dashed to pieces among the rocks and surging billows of this dreadful revolution.—New York Herald, April 22.

RETALIATION

The New York Courier and Enquirer, in an editorial, apparently from Gen. Webb's own hand, discourses as follows:—

"Most assuredly these madmen are calling down upon themselves a fearful retribution. We are no Abolitionists, as the columns of the Courier and Enquirer, for the whole period of its existence, now thirty-four years, will abundantly demonstrate. And for the whole of that period, except the first six months of its infancy, it has been under our exclusive editorial charge.

"Never, during that long period, has an Abolition sentiment found its way into our columns; and for the good reason, that we have respected, honored and revered the Constitution, and recognized our duty to obey and enforce its mandates. But Rebellion stalks through the land. A confederacy of slave States has repudiated that Constitution; and, placing themselves beyond its pale, openly seeks to destroy it, and ruin all whom it, protects. They no longer profess any obedience to its requirements; and, of course, cannot claim its protection. By their own act, our duty to respect their rights, under that Constitution, ceases with their repudiation of it; and our right to liberate their slave property is as clear as would be our right to liberate the slaves of Cuba in a war with Spain.

"A band of pirates threaten and authorize piracy upon Northern commerce; and from the moment that threat is carried into execution, the fetters will fall from the manacled limbs of their slaves, and they will be encouraged and aided in the establishment of their freedom. Suppose Cuba were to issue letters of marque against our commerce, and, according to the Charleston Mercury, seize 'upon the rich prizes which may be coming from foreign lands,' does any sane man doubt that we should at once invade that island, and liberate her slaves? Or does any statesman or jurist question our right so to do? And why, then, should we hesitate to pursue a similar course in respect to the so-called Southern Confederacy?

"Spain, as a well-established nation, and recognized as such by all the powers of the world, would have the right, according to the laws of nations, to adopt such a course of proceeding; but she would do it at her peril, and well weighing the consequences. But the rebel government of the slave States possesses no such right. The act would be no more or less than piracy; and we should not only hang at the yard-arm all persons caught in the practice, but we should be compelled, in self-defence, to carry the war into Africa, and deal with the slaves of the Confederacy precisely as we should, under similar circumstances, deal with those of Cuba.

"'The richly laden ships of the North,' says the Mobile Advertiser, 'swarm on every sea, and are absolutely unprotected. The harvest is ripe.' We admit it; but gather it if you dare. Venture upon the capture of the poorest of those richly laden ships,' and, from that moment, your slaves become freemen, doing battle in Freedom's cause. 'Hundreds and hundreds of millions of the property of the enemy invite us to spoil him—to spoil these Egyptians,' says the same paper. True, but you dare not venture upon the experiment; or, if you should be so rash as to make the experiment, your fourteen hundred millions of slave property will cease to exist, and you will find four millions of liberated slaves in your midst, wreaking upon their present masters the smothered vengeance of a servile race, who, for generation after generation, have groaned under the lash of the negro driver and his inhuman employer.

"'The risk of the privateer,' says the same organ of the rebel confederacy, 'will still be trifling; but he will continue to reap the harvest.' His risk will only be his neck, and his 'harvest' will be a halter. But the risk, nay, the certainty of the punishment to be visited upon the slave confederacy, will be far greater—of infinitely greater magnitude than they can well conceive; because it will be no more or less than the loss of all their slave property, accompanied with the necessity of contending, hand to hand, for their lives, with the servile race so long accustomed to the lash, and the torture, and the branding and maiming of their inhuman masters; a nation of robbers, who now, in the face of the civilized world, repudiate their just debts, rob banks and mints, sell freemen captured in an unarmed vessel into perpetual slavery, trample upon law and order, insult our flag, capture our forts and arsenals, and, finally, invite pirates to prey upon our commerce!

"Such a nest of pirates may do some mischief, and greatly alarm the timid. But the men of the North know how to deal with them; and we tell them, once for all, that, if they dare grant a solitary letter of marque, and the person or persons acting under it venture to assail the poorest of our vessels in the peaceful navigation of the ocean, or the coasts and rivers of our country—from that moment their doom is sealed, and slavery ceases to exist. We speak the unanimous sentiment of our people; and to that sentiment all in authority will be compelled to bow submissively. So let us hear no more of the idle gasconade of 'the Chivalry' of a nest of robbers, who seek to enlarge the area of their public and private virtues, &c."

This is very plain talk, and cannot easily be misapprehended by those whom it concerns.

O. A. BROWNSON ON THE WAR

There is neither reason nor justice in Massachusetts, New York, New Jersey, Pennsylvania and the great States northwest of the Ohio pouring out their blood and treasure for the gratification of the slaveholding pretensions of Maryland, Kentucky or Missouri. The citizens of these States who own slaves are as much bound, if the preservation of the Union requires it, to give up their property in slaves, as we at the farther North are to pour out our blood and treasure to put down a rebellion which threatens alike them and us. If they love their few slaves more than they do the Union, let them go out of the Union. We are stronger to fight the battles of the Union without them than we are with them.

But we have referred only to the slaves in the rebellious States, and if it is, or if it becomes, a military necessity to liberate all the slaves of the Union, and to treat the whole present slave population as freemen and citizens, it would be no more than just and proper that, at the conclusion of the war, the citizens of loyal States, or the loyal citizens of loyal sections of the rebellious States, should be indemnified at a reasonable rate for the slaves that may have been liberated. The States and sections of States named have not a large number of slaves, and if the Union is preserved, it would not be a very heavy burden on it to pay their ransom; and to paying it, no patriot or loyal citizen of the free States would raise the slightest objection. The objection therefore urged, though grave, need not be regarded as insuperable; and we think the advantages of the measure, in a military point of view, would be far greater than any disadvantage we have to apprehend from it.

Whether the time for this important measure has come or not, it is for the President, as Commander-in-Chief of our armies, to determine. But, in our judgment, no single measure could be adopted by the government that would more effectually aid its military operations, do more to weaken the rebel forces, and to strengthen our own.

It seems to us, then, highly important, in every possible view of the case, that the Federal Government should avail itself of the opportunity given it by the Southern rebellion to perform this act of justice to the negro race; to assimilate the labor system of the South to that of the North; to remove a great moral and political wrong; and to wipe out the foul stain of slavery, which has hitherto sullied the otherwise bright escutcheon of our Republic. We are no fanatics on the subject of slavery, as is well known to our readers, and we make no extraordinary pretensions to modern philanthropy; but we cannot help fearing that, if the government lets slip the present opportunity of doing justice to the negro race, and of placing our republic throughout in harmony with modern civilization, God, who is especially the God of the poor and the oppressed, will never give victory to our arms, or suffer us to succeed in our efforts to suppress rebellion and restore peace and integrity in the Union.

THE NEW YORK HERALD ON THE WAR

With the secession of Virginia, there is going to be enacted on the banks of the Potomac one of the most terrible conflicts the world has ever witnessed; and Virginia, with all her social systems, will be doomed, and swept away.—New York Herald, April 19.

We must also admonish the people of Maryland that we of the North have the common right of way through their State to our National Capital. But let her join the revolutionists, and her substance will be devoured by our Northern legions as by an Arabian cloud of locusts, and her slave population will disappear in a single campaign.

A Northern invasion of Virginia and of Kentucky, if necessary, carrying along with it the Canadian line of African freedom, as it must do from the very nature of civil war, will produce a powerful Union reaction. The slave population of the border States will be moved in two directions. One branch of it, without the masters, will be moved Northward, and the other branch, with the masters, will be moved Southward, so that, by the time the Northern army will have penetrated to the centre of the border slave States, they will be relieved of the substance and abstract rights of slave property for all time to come.

Finally, the revolted States having appealed to the sword of revolution to redress their wrongs, may soon have to choose between submission to the Union or the bloody extinction of slavery, from the absence of any law, any wish, any power for its protection.— Ibid, April 20.

By land and water, if she places herself in the attitude of rebellion, Maryland may be overrun and subdued in a single week, including the extinction of slavery within her own borders; for war makes its own laws.

We are less concerned about Washington than about Maryland. Loyal to the Union, she is perfectly safe, negroes and all; disloyal to the Union, she may be crushed, including her institution of slavery. Let her stand by the

Union, and the Union will protect and respect her— slavery and all.—Ibid, April 21.

Virginia, next to Maryland, will be subjected to this test. She has seceded, and hence she will probably risk the breaking of every bone in her body. If so, we fear that every bone in her body will be broken, including her backbone of slavery. The day is not far off when the Union men of the revolted States will be asked to come to the relief of their misguided brethren, for, otherwise, the war which they have chosen to secure their institution of slavery may result in wiping it out of existence.—Ibid, April 23.

In advance of this movement, President Lincoln should issue his proclamation, guaranteeing the complete protection of all loyal Union men and their property, but warning the enemies of the Government of the dangers of confiscation, negroes included.

If Virginia resists, the contest cannot last very long, considering her large slave population, which will either become fugitives or take up arms against their masters.—Ibid, April 24.

That we are to have a fight, that Virginia and Maryland will form the battle-ground, that the Northern roughs will sweep those States with fire and sword, is beyond peradventure. They have already been excited to the boiling point by the rich prospect of plunder held out by some of their leaders, and will not be satisfied unless they have a farm and a nigger each. There is no sort of exaggeration about these statements, as the people of the border States will shortly ascertain to their cost. The character of the coming campaign will be vindictive, fierce, bloody, and merciless beyond parallel in ancient or modern history.—Ibid, April 28.

The class of population which is recruiting in our large cities, the regiments forming for service in behalf of the Union, can never be permanently worsted. They will pour down upon the villages and cities of Virginia and Maryland, and leave a desolate track behind them, and inspire terror in whatever vicinity they approach.—Ibid, April 29.

It will be idle for Tennessee and Kentucky to attempt to escape from the issue, and to remain at peace, while the remainder of the country is at war. Neutrality will be considered opposition, and the result of a general frontier war will be, that slavery, as a domestic institution of the United States; will be utterly annihilated.—Ibid, April 30.

The rebellion must be put down by some means or another, else it will put us down; and if nothing else will do, even to proclaim the abolition of slavery would be legitimate. All is fair in war…Gen. Fremont and the other Generals must act according to circumstances, and their own judgment, unless when otherwise ordered…If he is acting on his own responsibility, he is only carrying out the Confiscation Act, so far as the slaves are concerned… We have no fear of the result.—N. Y. Herald, Sept. 3.

BUT ONE WAY OUT

To our apprehension, God is fast closing every avenue to settled peace but by emancipation. And one of the most encouraging facts is that the eyes of the nation are becoming turned in that direction quite as rapidly as could have been anticipated. Some men of conservative antecedents, like Dickinson of New York, saw this necessity from the first. But it takes time to accustom a whole people to the thought, and to make them see the necessity. It was impossible for Northern men to fathom the spirit and the desperate exigencies of the slave system and its outbreak, and consequently to comprehend the desperate nature of the struggle. We were like a policeman endeavoring to arrest a boy-ruffian, and, for the sake of his friends and for old acquaintance sake, doing it with all possible tenderness for his person and his feelings—till all of a sudden he feels the grip on his throat and the dagger's point at his breast, and knows that it is a life-and-death grapple.

Slaveholding is simply piracy continued. Our people are beginning to spell out that short and easy lesson in the light of perjury, robbery, assassination, poisoning, and all the more than Algerine atrocities of this rebellion. It cannot require many more months of schooling like the last eight, to convince the dullest of us what are its essence and spirit.

Our people also are rapidly finding out that no peaceful termination of this war will be permitted now by the Slave Power, except by its thorough overthrow. The robber has thrown off the mask, and says now to the nation, "Your life or mine!" Even the compromising Everett has boldly told the South, "To be let alone is not all you ask—but you demand a great deal more." And in his late oration, he has most powerfully portrayed the impossibility of a peaceful disunion. Many men, some anti-slavery, were at first inclined to yield to the idea of a separation. But every day's experience is scattering that notion to the winds. The ferocious spirit exhibited from the first by the Secessionists towards all dissentients, the invasion of Western Virginia by Eastern, the threats to put down loyal Kentucky, the foray in Missouri, the plan for capturing Washington, which was part of the original scheme, are convincing proofs, that if by any pacification whatever our troops were disbanded to-day, to-morrow a Southern army would be on the march for Washington, Philadelphia, New York, and perhaps Chicago.

The South has sufficiently declared the cause of this trouble to be the irreconcilable conflict between their institutions and the fundamental principles of this government. While the cause remains in full strength, and after it has once burst forth in bloody and final collision, nothing will ever check that strife, whether in or out of the Union. The cause must be eradicated. Meanwhile, our own position, both before the world and in our own struggle at home, is a false one, so long as we blink the real issue.

Many indications are hopeful. Gen. Butler's letter to the Secretary of War, and the Secretary's reply, look in the right direction. The Confiscation Act is pregnant with great consequences, and may yet be so used as to become an emancipation act in all the rebel States. It is high time it were so used. We have serious doubts whether the rebellion will ever be suppressed till that trenchant weapon is wielded. We reverently doubt whether the Lord means it shall be. The quiet passage of the Confiscation Act was an immense step of governmental progress. Perhaps it was all that the nation as a whole and the government were ready for. It may answer as a keen wedge. But we trust that, in December, Congress will make clean work by the full emancipation of all slaves in the rebel States, and by provision in some way for the speedy and certain extinction of slavery in the loyal States. To accomplish the latter event, we would ourselves willingly submit to any proper amount of pecuniary burden, provided it could be so arranged as not to recognize a right of property in man. — Chicago Congregational Herald.

PROCLAMATION OF GEN. FREMONT

HEADQUARTERS, WESTERN DIVISION,
St. Louis, Aug. 30, 1861.

Circumstances; in my judgment, are of sufficient urgency to render it necessary that the Commanding General of this Department should assume administrative powers of the State. Its disorganized condition, helplessness of civil authority, and the total insecurity of life and devastation of property by bands of murderers and marauders, who infest nearly every county in the State, and avail themselves of public misfortunes and the vicinity of a hostile force to gratify private and neighborhood vengeance, and who find an enemy wherever they find plunder, finally demand the severest measures to repress the daily increasing crimes and outrages which are driving off the inhabitants and ruining the State. In this condition, the public safety and the success of our arms require unity of purpose, without let or hindrance, to the prompt administration of affairs. In order, therefore, to suppress disorder, maintain the public peace, and give security to the persons and property of loyal citizens, I do hereby extend and declare martial law throughout the State of Missouri.

The lines of the army occupation in this State are, for the present, declared to extend from Leavenworth by way of posts to Jefferson City, Rolla and Ironton, to Cape Girardeau, on the Mississippi river. All persons who shall be taken with arms in their hands, within these lines, shall be tried by court martial, and, if found guilty, shall be shot.

Real and personal property, owned by persons who shall take up arms against the United States, or who shall be directly proven to have taken an active part with the enemy in the field, is declared confiscated to public use, and their slaves, if any they have, are hereby declared free men. All persons who shall be proven to, have destroyed, after the publication of this order, railroad tracks, bridges or telegraph lines, shall suffer the extreme penalty of the law. All persons engaged in treasonable correspondence, in giving or procuring aid to the enemy, in fomenting turmoils and disturbing public tranquility by creating or circulating false reports or incendiary documents, are warned that they are exposing themselves. All persons who have been led away from allegiance are requested to return to their homes forthwith.

Any such absence, without sufficient cause, will be held to be presumptive evidence against them.

The object of this declaration is to place in the hands of the military authorities power to give instantaneous effect to the existing laws, and to supply such deficiencies as the conditions of the war demand; but it is not intended to suspend the ordinary tribunals of the country where law will be administered by civil officers in the usual manner, and with their customary authority, while the same can be peaceably administered.

The Commanding General will labor vigilantly for the public welfare, and, by his efforts for their safety, hopes to obtain not only acquiescence, but the active support of the people of the country.

(Signed,)

J. C. FREMONT,
Major General Commanding.

SLAVERY HAS DONE IT

Let us not for one moment lose sight of this fact. We go into this war not merely to sustain the government and defend the Constitution. There is a moral principle involved. How came that government in danger? What has brought this wicked war, with all its evils and horrors, upon us? Whence comes the necessity for this uprising of the people? To these questions, there can be but one answer. SLAVERY HAS DONE IT. That accursed system, which has already cost us so much, has at length culminated in this present ruin and confusion. That system must be put down. The danger must never be suffered to occur again. The evil must be eradicated, cost what it may. We are for no half-way measures. So long as the slave system kept itself within the limits of the Constitution, we were bound to let it alone, and to respect its legal rights; but when, overleaping those limits, it bids defiance to all law, and lays its vile hands on the sacred altar of liberty and the sacred flag of the country, and would overturn the Constitution itself, thenceforth slavery has no constitutional rights. It is by its own act an outlaw. It can never come back again into the temple, and claim a place by right among the worshippers of truth and liberty. It has ostracised itself, and that for ever.

Let us not be told, then, that the matter of slavery does not enter into the present controversy—that it is merely a war to uphold the government and put down secession. It is not so. So far from this, slavery is the very heart and head of this whole struggle. The conflict is between freedom on the one hand, maintaining its rights, and slavery on the other, usurping and demanding that to which it has no right. It is a war of principle as well as of self-preservation; and that is but a miserable and short-sighted policy which looks merely at the danger and overlooks the cause; which seeks merely to put out the fire, and lets the incendiary go at large, to repeat the experiment at his leisure. We must do both—put out the fire, and put out the incendiary too. We meet the danger effectually only by eradicating the disease.—Erie True American.

THE SLAVES AS A MILITARY ELEMENT

The total white population of the eleven States now comprising the confederacy is six million, and, therefore, to fill up the ranks of the proposed army (600,000) about ten percent of the entire white population will be required. In any other country than our own, such a draft could not be met, but the Southern States can furnish that number of men, and still not leave the material interests of the country in a suffering condition. Those who are incapacitated for bearing arms can oversee the plantations, and the negroes can go on undisturbed in their usual labors. In the North, the case is different; the men who join the army of subjugation are the laborers, the producers, and the factory operatives. Nearly every man from that section, especially those from the rural districts, leaves some branch of industry to suffer during his absence. The institution of slavery in the South alone enables her to place in the field a force much larger in proportion to her white population than the North, or indeed any country which is dependent entirely on free labor. The institution is a tower of strength to the South, particularly at the present crisis, and our enemies will be likely to find that the "moral cancer," about which their orators are so fond of prating, is really one of the most effective weapons employed against the Union by the South. Whatever number of men may be needed for this war, we are confident our people stand ready to furnish. We are all enlisted for the war, and there must be no holding back until the independence of the South is fully acknowledged.—Montgomery (Ala.) Adv.

A NOVEL SIGHT

A procession of several hundred stout negro men, members of the "domestic institution," marched through our streets yesterday in military order, under the command of Confederate officers. They were well armed and equipped with shovels, axes, blankets, &c. A merrier set never were seen. They were brimful of patriotism, shouting for Jeff. Davis and singing war songs, and each looked as if he only wanted the privilege of shooting an Abolitionist.

An Abolitionist could not have looked upon this body of colored recruits for the Southern army without strongly suspecting that his intense sympathy for the "poor slave" was not appreciated, that it was wasted on an ungrateful subject.

The arms of these colored warriors were rather mysterious. Could it be that those gleaming axes were intended to drive into the thick skulls of the Abolitionists the truth, to which they are wilfully blind, that their interference in behalf of Southern slaves is neither appreciated nor desired; or that those shovels were intended to dig trenches for the interment of their carcasses? It may be that the shovels are to be used in digging ditches, throwing up breastworks, or the construction of masked batteries, those abominations to every abolition Paul Pry who is so unlucky as to stumble upon them.—Memphis Avalanche, Sept. 3.

Notes

www.ingramcontent.com/pod-product-compliance
Lightning Source LLC
LaVergne TN
LVHW041445170726
843492LV00008B/2812